Ethnographic Terminalia: New Orleans 2010
DuMois Gallery

Published by the Society for Visual Anthropology, a section of the
American Anthropological Association. 2300 Clarendon Blvd.,
Suite 1301. Arlington, VA 22201

Review essays in this volume were originally published in the journal Visual
Anthropology Review. Our grateful acknowledgement to the editors.

Edited by Ethnographic Terminalia:
Craig Campbell, Kate Hennessy, Fiona P. McDonald, Trudi Lynn Smith,
Stephanie Takaragawa

Lead editors and print design: Kate Hennessy and Rachel Topham

Exhibition Photography: Ethnographic Terminalia

Cover Design: Ethnographic Terminalia, Rachel Topham and
Ian Kirkpatrick

ISBN 978-1-931303-49-1

New Orleans 2010:

Contributors

Ethnographic Terminalia

New Orleans 2010

Du Mois Gallery

2010 Principal Curator
Craig Campbell

Partnering Curator
Maria Brodine

Co-Curators
Kate Hennessy
Fiona P. McDonald
Trudi Lynn Smith
Stephanie Takaragawa

Acknowledgements

The second iteration of Ethnographic Terminalia was installed in two locations: the main exhibit space was an historic shotgun house (turned gallery) in the Freret district, and two works were mounted in an eclectic space in the St. Claude Art District. We would like to acknowledge and extend deep appreciation to The Du Mois Gallery and Barrister's Gallery for the dynamic spaces to work within. Maria Brodine provided on the ground connections to the community and Ethnographic Terminalia greatly benefitted from working to support Brodine's Art Spill: Disaster, Art, Activism, and Recovery in Post-Katrina New Orleans. Volunteer Rowan Campbell helped with the installation of the works.

Support was provided by The American Anthropological Association's Community Engagement Fund, The Society for Visual Anthropology, The Americo Paredes Center for Cultural Studies (University of Texas at Austin), and The School of Interactive Arts and Technology (Simon Fraser University). We would like to thank Stella Artois and San Pellergrino and especially extend our thanks to Jerry Peters of Southern Eagle Sales and Services. We would like to express our sincere appreciation to all of the artists who provided documentation for us to review. Finally, we would like to thank the artists in Ethnographic Terminalia both for their work and for their participation.

General installation view, New Orleans, 2010.

General installation view, New Orleans, 2010.

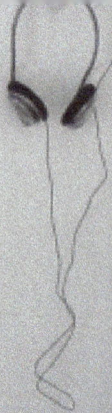

General installation view, New Orleans, 2010.

General installation view, New Orleans, 2010.

Ethnographic Terminalia
NEW ORLEANS 2010

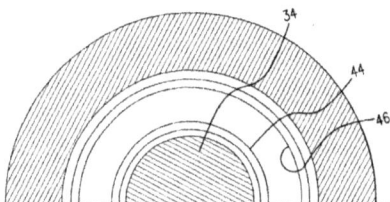

ETHNOGRAPHIC TERMINALIA:

AN INTRODUCTION

Maria Brodine, Craig Campbell, Kate Hennessy

Fiona P. McDonald, Trudi Lynn Smith, and Stephanie Takaragawa

*The terminus is the end, the boundary, and the border; the terminus is also a beginning,
as well as its own place, its own site of experience and encounter—a space of
anthropological and artistic inquiry.*

Ethnographic Terminalia was originally conceived in response to the lack of
opportunity for either anthropologists working as artists or artists engaging
with anthropology to present their work in, adjacent to, or in tension with
scholarly contexts. In the last two years, Ethnographic Terminalia has grown
through collaboration between an emerging curatorial collective and partnering
exhibitors into an ongoing project. Our goal is to generate a space that connects
anthropology and art together in new ways, and to contribute to the ongoing
dialogue between anthropology and art in practice. The collective takes this to
task beyond the more traditional scholarly channels. Therefore, Ethnographic
Terminalia is an initiative designed to celebrate borders without necessarily
exalting them. As a platform from which divergent modes and methodologies
of inquiry are articulated, the collective asks what lies beyond and lies within
disciplinary territories. As an imaginative project, it is meant to be a serious play
with reflexivity and positionality.

Reprinted with permission. Brodine, Maria, Craig Campbell, Kate Hennessy, Fiona P. McDonald,
Trudi Lynn Smith, Stephanie Takaragawa. 2011 Ethnographic Terminalia: An Introduction.
Visual Anthropology Review 27(1):49-51.

Background

As a collective project, Ethnographic Terminalia offers a curated forum for researchers, artists, and anthropologists to share ideas and create dialogues about divergent methodologies and practices employed in current research projects. The space that is created by Ethnographic Terminalia allows artists and anthropologists to present their projects and their research methodologies, and subsequently coexist for a larger public to experience.

The space that is generated in this project extends beyond the walls of any specific gallery. It is designed to allow artists and anthropologists an environment within which they can present their work (techniques, research methodologies, modes of expression, etc.). This environment subsequently offers multiple entries and invitations, allowing different publics a variety of points of access. Therefore, as a curatorial methodology the collective continually seeks out unique exhibition spaces, modes of display, and practices of facilitation.

In the last two years, a curatorial group has emerged, consisting of the authors of this introduction, who are committed to developing and refining the modes of opportunity for Ethnographic Terminalia as a project that creates space for experimentation, exhibition, critique, and conversation alongside the annual meetings of the American Anthropological Association (AAA). The group has worked collectively to organize, curate, and mount exhibitions in Philadelphia (2009) and New Orleans (2010), with a subgroup of Ethnographic Terminalia each year taking on principal curatorial roles. These exhibitions were created in cooperation with a local partnering curator who liaised with our host gallery and brought invaluable skills as mediator and facilitator of the development of a context-sensitive relationship to the local artistic and academic community. The first iteration of Ethnographic Terminalia took place in 2009 in Philadelphia at Crane Arts, occupying the Ice Box Gallery, the Grey Area, and the Media Room. The exhibition's Principal Curators were Craig Campbell and Fiona P. McDonald, with Partnering Local Curator Annabelle Rodriguez, and Co-Organizers Kate Hennessy and Stephanie Takagarawa. Works exhibited in this first show were invited from an emerging network of artist-ethnographers and ethnographer-artists, who, like the members of the curatorial collective, were seeking a venue for nontextual ethnographic articulations. With their participation, the collective was able to establish a framework that subsequently responded to those within the community of international anthropologists seeking an alternative space to present their research. The scope of works from site-specific installation works, video, documentary, photography, interactive media, material culture, sound works, and performance offered up a multisensorial experience that originated in the academic discipline of anthropology but moved beyond to community collaboration and participation. Together, 17 artists and anthropologists were represented in conversation that responded to the 108th AAA meeting's theme of boundaries and the ends of the discipline.

The momentum of Ethnographic Terminalia continued into 2010 as a new exhibition was mounted at the Du Mois Gallery and Barrister's Gallery in New Orleans. The exhibition was curated by Craig Campbell (Principal Curator) and Maria Brodine (Partnering Local Curator), and co-organized by Kate Hennessy, Fiona P. McDonald, Trudi Lynn Smith, and Stephanie Takaragawa. The works of Susan Hiller, Fiamma Montezemolo, and Robert Willim and Anders Weberg were invited to be the anchor pieces from which a call for submissions was released. The curatorial collective selected over 20 additional works out of over 70 responses to an international open artist call inviting submissions. As described in the 2010 call for submissions:

> The works exhibited in Ethnographic Terminalia emerge through a desire to produce art as a process or product of research. As we demonstrated in the Ethnographic Terminalia 2009 exhibition, the juxtaposition of works that bear nothing more in common than loose disciplinary or discursive histories—languages of observation and description—produces what might be analogously seen as a contemporary cabinet of curiosities. The works exist and generate their own logical structures as autonomous units but they are also part of a larger collection, accruing and developing meaning through proximity to other works. In this case the curatorial task of locating the various works in the gallery is critical.

With a mandate to network within a closely-knit arts community of New Orleans, the curators included works that addressed the place and community of New Orleans. Ethnographic Terminalia also supported related events Art Spill: Disaster, Art, Activism, and Recovery and SWARM: Multispecies Salon III, which are described in Maria Brodine's essay in this issue.

In addition to the exhibitions, informal art critiques with artists and anthropologists involved in the exhibition were held at the end of the 2009 and 2010 exhibitions. Rather than deconstructing the formal qualities of each project, participants have used this forum as an opportunity to share the nuanced details of their work that subsequently produces fodder for further problematizing key issues that link art and anthropology. As a part of the official program of the 2010 Annual Meeting of the AAA, a roundtable discussion called "Ethnographic Termini: Moving and Agitating within the Borderlands of Contemporary Art and Ethnography" featured the perspectives and work of a selection of participating artists and local curators. Those who participated on the roundtable were Craig Campbell, Tarek Elhaik, Fiamma Montezemolo, Morgana King, Nicky Levell, Michael Nicoll Yahgulanaas, and Thomas Ross Miller.

Upon reflection, the significant response to our call for artists to show in Ethnographic Terminalia in New Orleans coupled with the active engagement of participants and visitors has reaffirmed our awareness of the need for artists and anthropologists to muster in spaces such as the Ethnographic Terminalia project. To carry forward this generative space and present a divergent scope of work, the Montréal 2011 exhibition will also circulate a general call for submissions.

References

American Anthropology Association, Society for Visual Anthropology
    2010   Ethnographic Terminalia 2010, New Orleans: Call for
              Participation. http://societyforvisualanthropolog.org/?p=1236,
              accessed January 20, 2011.

Ethnographic Terminalia Homepage.
              www.ethnographic terminalia.org, accessed January 21, 2011.

Ethnographic Terminalia 2010: New Orleans
    2010   Exhibition Catalog. New Orleans: Du Mois Gallery.

Ethnographic Terminalia 2011
    2011   Prospectus. www.ethnographicterminalia.org,
              accessed January 20, 2011.

ETHNOGRAPHIC TERMINALIA:
TERMINUS

Craig Campbell

"Terminus" reflects on the curatorial impetus behind the 2010 Ethnographic Terminalia show, held in New Orleans.

Terminus: The point to which motion or action tends . . . sometimes that from which it starts . . .[1]

I sat in the fourth room of the Du Mois Gallery, a long shotgun-style house in New Orleans, on four separate occasions to watch Susan Hiller's *Last Silent Movie.* The audio bounced around the small room and voices worked to raise the hair on my neck several times. I like gallery works of long duration. At least I like the idea of them, I like the implicit lack of expectation that I must experience the whole thing in one sitting, or enter in to the watching at a specific moment. It is rare that I find myself in the right space or moment for taking them in. There is a weight to the Hiller work that presses my attention closely to it. The mostly unfamiliar languages tend to have an effect of slipping into the background of consciousness but the matter-of-fact presentation of the translation is a hook to my attention. It sets the tone for the room and echoes through the gallery.

Reprinted with permission. Campbell, Craig. 2011 Terminus: Ethnographic Terminalia. Visual Anthropology Review 27(1):52-56.

Ethnographic Terminalia (ET) is a project aimed at fostering art-based practices among anthropologists and other cultural investigators or critics. It accomplishes this mission through the organization of exhibitions and workshops. A series of exhibitions is currently underway with support from the American Anthropological Association and the Society for Visual Anthropology. These exhibitions are timed to coincide with the annual meetings of the American Anthropological Association—an event that draws thousands of attendees (over 5,000 in 2009). The first exhibition was held in Philadelphia at Crane Arts in 2009. This show brought together 17 exhibitors (both anthropologists and artists). The 2010 exhibition was mounted in New Orleans at two galleries (Du Mois and Barrister's). A third exhibition is planned for Montréal, Canada, in 2011.

Ethnographic Terminalia 2010: New Orleans had multiple threads woven together through efforts to speak simultaneously to the broad membership of the American Anthropological Association and the Society for Visual Anthropology, as well as an even narrower community of visual anthropologists interested in contemporary art. But these mobile and largely nonlocal individuals are only part of the conversation. The other people addressed are contemporary artists, patrons of contemporary art, as well as the local community (who are interested or affiliated by dint of proximity to the gallery). These people might be said to comprise one of Ethnographic Terminalia's publics—that grouping of nonspecialists who exist largely outside the specific language or jargon and theoretical and political currents of academic cultural critique. It is in the possibilities provided by the art gallery as a genre of experience that allows us to engage various publics, constituted across specific interests. As a conceptual platform, Ethnographic Terminalia supports a coalescence of activities and actors. It secures a space of emergence (or potential emergence) through a loose participatory organization convened around the activities of looking, showing, and discussing.

Participating in the curatorial vision for Ethnographic Terminalia has been driven by an effort to negotiate an emergent identity for gallery-based visual anthropology amid a raft of competing and contested institutions and practices. The meetings of the American Anthropological Association itself are evidence of this. Where the institutional framework provides the possibility of a sizable audience, it also necessitates a forfeiture of formal attention to corporate offerings. Visual anthropology, possibly more than any other subdiscipline, has suffered from this with substandard projection systems, antiquated equipment, and regrettable audio. The experience, especially for filmmakers, is underwhelming and often disappointing. While members of the Society for Visual Anthropology have labored to make the events as good as possible, they are working against a structure that is largely uninterested in formal qualities of experience–or at least one that has resigned itself to suffering the mediocrity of American halls of assembly. The specific needs of visual anthropologists in most convention centers will never be more than an afterthought.

Ethnographic Terminalia 2010: New Orleans presented itself as a constellation of events, a structure engineered to accommodate different visions and possibilities. Understanding the relationship of the various nodes to one another as informal and sometimes haphazard should not, however, preclude a recognition of them as autonomous points of intensity and emergence. There were five principal nodes in the Ethnographic Terminalia 2010: New Orleans exhibition: Du Mois Gallery, Barrister's Gallery, Art Spill, Ethnographic Termini round table, and the Ethnographic Terminalia website.

The Du Mois Gallery became the central point in the constellation of ET-related events. With 23 projects, the Du Mois Gallery was turned entirely over to the work of artists, anthropologists, and collaborative teams. Anchoring the show was Susan Hiller's *The Last Silent Movie*, Robert Willim and Anders Weberg's *Elsewhereness: New Orleans*, and Fiamma Montezemolo's *Belonging Machine: Color by Chance*, *One Thing AND Another*, and *Tijuana Bio Cartography*. The Du Mois Gallery is an independently run commercial gallery, operated by Renee Deville and Jean-Paul Villere.

Ethnographic Terminalia positioned two works at Barrister's Gallery: Ryan Burns's *Profane Relics* and Lina Dib's *Recantorium*. The location of Burns's piece could not be more perfect. The yard at Barrister's Gallery offered a kind of open antechamber for the alcove that hosts Burns's work. The detritus and waste of Burns's ficto- archaeology provide a powerful counterpoint to Lina Dib's interactive work on the mundane affects surrounding the collection and accumulation of things. Barrister's Gallery is run by the curator Andy Antippas and is located in the St. Claude arts district, which is also the locale of the third node, Art Spill. Art Spill emerged as a project after Ethnographic Terminalia had already begun to curate the show at Du Mois. Following Maria Brodine's enthusiasm, Art Spill produced a dialogue between anthropology, art, and activism. With an official AAA-sponsored event an Art Spill panel discussion helped to situate the art works. Maria discusses Art Spill at greater length in this edition.

While Ethnographic Terminalia seeks to operate as a para-site to the American Anthropological Association meetings, it is also designed to engage specifically with the community of anthropologists who gather each year under the banner of the AAA. This year Maria Brodine and Craig Campbell organized an invited round table sponsored by the Council on Anthropology and Education and the Society for Visual Anthropology. From the round table abstract:

> The lecture hall, the project space, the gallery, the class room, the space of the monograph or the journal, subversive spaces, the website: all of these, are imagined within a discursive geography of connections and non-connections. The goal here is to bring artists, ethnographers, and curators into close proximity to see what happens when their discursive approaches brush up against one another. This notion of proximity must also be central to the guiding theme of the conference: circulations. This roundtable is in its own way performative of circulations. As a generative project it reflects the larger program of Ethnographic Terminalia, which is to hasten and amplify circulations between different creative actors.

Participants in the round table included Tarek Elhaik, Fiamma Montezemolo, Morgana King, Nicky Levell, Michael Nicoll Yahgulanaas, Thomas Ross Miller, and Craig Campbell.
Finally, it is important to recognize the crucial role played by the Ethnographic Terminalia website as a node in our constellation. Not only has the website

provided a means of communicating details about the exhibitions, but it also serves as an archive of the show and thus works toward the development of greater recognition for works of visual anthropology. Ethnographic Terminalia was created not only to provide a venue to show works (to our peers and to others) but also to parlay the event into greater academic currency. The website is thus not merely a tool for promotion but an archive for legitimation.

> The terminus is the end, the boundary, and the border; of course the terminus is also a beginning as well as its own place, its own site of experience and encounter.

Ethnographic Terminalia has been a boundary-work project—an investigatory and ultimately generative effort. A focus on rhetorical, political, and disciplinary conventions extends beyond the study of visual regimes or systems to encompass the challenge of producing art exhibitions that are in dialogue with contemporary anthropological discourse. There is a danger in folding the truth claims of intellectual research into the often vague and ambiguous milieu of the white (or black)-cube gallery. In 2009 and 2010, this danger is cultivated not only in the choice to exhibit works in a gallery space but to exhibit them in a way that eschews thematic oversight and that mimics one of the obscene forms of colonial exoticism: the *wunderkammer*.

Wunderkammer as Curatorial Principle

Where conventional academic monographs are designed to illuminate and provide historical clarity, art gallery space provides interpretive frictions that can impede and confound interpretation. The curatorial approach for the 2009 and 2010 exhibitions was aimed at agitating the experience of documentary clarity and was designed to produce an effect that places the spectator in a position of relative uncertainty vis-à-vis the larger project. In this cabinet of wonder, the operational logic is montage that lends itself to uncertainty about the overarching meaning: discerning one project from the next, as well as curatorial intent from convenience. While each exhibited work is self-contained, they are all made to speak on (or within) another register where new, possibly unexpected—even unwanted—meanings might be generated through juxtaposition and contextual shift. Such a montage as a curatorial principle rejects overt formulations and, following Walter Benjamin, is designed to allow the individual works to come into their own, without subsuming them into any obvious framework (Benjamin 1999:460; N1a, 8). Benjamin's approach to literary montage was meant to be carefully orchestrated and constructed, just as Dziga Vertov assembled *Man With a Movie Camera* (1929), but it also leaves something to intuition. The naïveté of intuition is both dangerous and attractive as it is an unformed thought observed at a moment of emergence but neither caught nor completely explained. Assembling the exhibitions for Ethnographic Terminalia balanced such sensibilities but was ultimately driven by a desire to let each work have a place of its own.

In *Collectors and Curiosities* (1990), Krzysztof Pomian notes the role of curiosity in the wunderkammer. He writes that the wunderkammer "was a universe to which corresponded a type of curiosity no longer controlled by theology and not yet controlled by science, both these domains tending to reject certain questions as either blasphemous or impertinent, thus subjecting curiosity to a discipline and imposing certain limits on it" (originally cited in Yanni 2005:16). The metaphor of the wunderkammer as an interval of formal curiosity carries forward to this particular moment in the development of visual anthropology. That its appetites are shifting, we might be said to be in an era when anthropological curiosity is no longer controlled by science, nor is it controlled by narrow politics of representation (i.e., being driven by pedagogy rather than critique).

While each artist is free to frame his or her own work, we have insisted that there are some traces and linkages provided to visitors in the gallery. Unwilling, in most cases, to relinquish all explanatory authority, the curatorial collective sought to provide some interpretive direction without making it the primary means of contact between the spectator and the work. Interpretive direction, then, is a rough principle of limits rather than a walled garden of hermeneutic possibility. The catalog for the show functioned as a reference point between each statement and its corresponding work, indexed by the name of the exhibitor. The catalog as a companion to the exhibition meant that we produced two archives in parallel, allowing for the performative cross-indexing of words and works. This formula of companion pieces reduced the subordination of one to the other. Some visitors engaged with the works outside of any particular reference to the catalog and its textual framing and exposition. Others began with the catalog and then sought out particular exhibitors or works. Multiple points of engagement with each exhibitor's project generated a textured and layered experience, producing multifaceted points of engagement for each contribution.

Ethnographic Terminalia has been an opportunistic project with broad categorical imperatives. The simple desire to find a place to show boundary-oblivious works of research-based art or intermedia ethnography has generally disregarded the formalities and politics of museums and galleries. Without being naïve to the critiques of institutionalized ideologies of museums and galleries, Ethnographic Terminalia has entered into these sites in a spirit of experimentation. The use of the word *terminalia* plays on the linguistic implication of *term*, such as disciplinary terms and terms of art, suggesting a question like "what are the terms of ethnography?" But more importantly, terminalia invokes the Latin word terminus: the limit or the end. *Terminalia* itself refers to a festival celebrated in ancient Rome on the 23rd of February. It was a ritual marking the boundaries between one demarcated territory and another. It is said that landowners made sacrifices at zones of abutment, erecting statues and stone markers in honor of the god Terminus. Whatever it was then, today we are left with this word that suggests primarily the end of something and the beginning of another thing. Where one thing ends another one begins. In the spirit of the *frontera*, of works that have been of critical importance to me (Gloria Anzaldua's *Frontera* work [1987]; Ann Fienup-Riordan's brilliant ethnography of Eskimo cosmology, *Boundaries and Passages* [1994]), the liminal is a supremely productive and interesting zone. Where does something cease to be ethnography, or anthropology? What are its limits? Occupying the space between, rather than a canonical center, seems to be both productive and dangerous.

In the name of this project "ethnography" is meant in the broadest of ways and is designated as a signifier of cultural study, analysis, critique, and expression. It is an ethnography that is open to other voices, one that refuses the narrow orthodoxy of Malinowskian practices; the methodology of long-term fieldwork in far-flung places.[2] In any event it is the -*graphy*, the writing of culture, that interests me more at this point than does the analytic and methodological prescriptions surrounding the study of culture and ethnos. And it is precisely the imagining of what ethnography can be, might be (or might have been) that drives this project. Ethnographic Terminalia is an exploration of definitions, borders, boundaries, edges, frontiers, and margins. It is premised on the idea that what lies beyond the ethnographic monograph is interesting and inherently valuable. As such it is a project concerned with form and the aesthetics of ethnographic representations. While the conceptualization of objects of study might be taken for granted (as a question of professionalization or disciplinary socialization), it is largely the point of expression that is of interest in this anthropology inter-media.

The name Ethnographic Terminalia, then, is a good place to end. With the publication of a small raft of books on art and ethnography and a growing number of tenured and tenure-track anthropologists engaged in producing nonconformist visual anthropology, there is an acute pressure for recognition by the profession at large and, more importantly, in the academy.

Notes

[1] 'terminus, n." OED Online. November 2010. Oxford University Press. http://www.oed.com.ezproxy.lib.utexas.edu/view/ Entry/199440, accessed January 12, 2011.

[2] As Bruce Albert noted in *Critique of Anthropology* over a decade ago, "the founding mythology of Malinowskian fieldwork continues to haunt anthropology's imaginary" (Albert 1997:53). By no means is it a denigration of this, though. I still hold fieldwork and slow scholarship as an ideal of committed and ethical research practice.

References

Albert, Bruce

    1997   'Ethnographic Situation' and Ethnic Movements: Notes on Post-Malinowskian Fieldwork. Critique of Anthropology 17(1):53–65.

Anzaldúa, Gloria

    1987   Borderlands/La Frontera: The New Mestiza. 1st edition. San Francisco: Spinsters/Aunt Lute.

Benjamin, Walter

    1999   Walter Benjamin: Selected Writings, Volume 2, 1927– 1934. Cambridge, MA: The Belknap Press of Harvard University Press.

Fienup-Riordan, Ann

    1994   Boundaries and Passages: Rule and Ritual in Yup'ik Eskimo Oral Tradition. Norman: University of Oklahoma Press.

Pomian, Krzysztof

    1990   Collectors and Curiosities: Paris and Venice 1500– 1800. Cambridge: Polity Press.

Vertov, Dziga, dir.

    1929   The Man with a Movie Camera. New York: Kino Video.

Yanni, Carla

    2005   Nature's Museums: Victorian Science and the Architecture of Display. New York: Princeton Architectural Press.

NEW ORLEANS 2010:

27 WORKS

Kate Hennessy, Fiona P. McDonald, Trudi Lynn Smith,

Stephanie Takaragawa

The projects presented in Ethnographic Terminalia 2010: New Orleans—*27 Works* contextualize each work within the 2010 exhibition installed in New Orleans at the Du Mois Gallery. The summary of each project in this article captures the methodology of research that informs the conversation between art and anthropology, as well as demonstrating the full scope of the exhibition that includes works from film to photography, material culture, installation, and participatory works. Artists' bios are coupled with their own commentary on the nuanced details of how the projects relate to the discourses of art and anthropology. This article is also used to situate the curatorial goals of the Ethnographic Terminalia collective to move beyond the exhibition catalog in order to archive the project in an alternative form.

The works exhibited in Ethnographic Terminalia 2010: New Orleans represent a diversity of material, conceptual, and creative engagements with art and anthropology. The projects described below capture the multiplicity of methodologies and mediums, from post-studio practice, to sound installation, drawing, sculpture, photography and video works.

Hennessy, Kate, Fiona P. McDonald, Trudi Lynn Smith, Stephanie Takaragawa.
2011 Ethnographic Terminalia 2010: New Orleans—27 Works.
Visual Anthropology Review 27(1):57-74.

The two-dimensional works curated in Ethnographic Terminalia 2010: New Orleans ranged from drawings including hand-notated architectural drafts, to digital prints of color fields, black-and-white graphic panels, and photographs. Photography had a prominent place in the exhibition, with different artists deploying the medium in varied manners. While one project presents black-and-white documentary photographs, another project is characterized by warm-toned black-and-white historical postcards. Several artists used large-scale color photographs that ranged in size from 18 to 36 inches. As an approach to ethnographic inquiry and the anthropological subject, these works record an observation, tell a story, act as performance, and reflect community engagement, as well as question photographic distance, probing the boundaries of truth and fiction, presence and absence. The engagement with photography as both a means of inquiry and as a mode of expression is represented in the diverse engagements with thismedium, from works intended to be viewed on the wall to those spilling onto a table to be sorted and handled by visitors.

Moving into three-dimensional space, several works explicitly dealt with materiality and material culture in tangible ways. Ethnographic Terminalia 2010: New Orleans exhibited site-specific installations that coupled community participation through projects that were contextualized in the gallery space proper. Interactive works enabled visitor participation and subsequently played with a range of approaches, from technologically sophisticated media art, to low-tech found objects remixed into participatory sound works. The curators displayed interactive works alongside small and large-scale archaeology projects as sculptural installations, which were contrasted against sound installations that were composed of traces that drew upon documentation and interpretation of the locality of New Orleans.

Works in video highlighted a range of creative engagements with the medium. While one project presented archival sound recordings with subtitles, another experimented with single silent video take. One eschewed translation, while another featured subtitled narrative in tension with revolving images. Visual and sound montage coupled with layers of digital artifacts of analog transmission contrast with the integration of found photographs and speculative reminiscences. Each reflects the purposing of video in the articulation of an anthropological theme or reference; each speaks to the broader project of reconciling artistic practice, archival production, and ethnographic inquiry with rapidly evolving digital tools and aesthetic potentials. Several of the video works arrived at the DuMois Gallery in their own portable media players, and were exhibited as they had been shipped: mobile, exploratory, prepared for an audience.

The following descriptions of the works presented in Ethnographic Terminalia 2010: New Orleans are presented as they were curated in both the Du Mois gallery space and Barrister's Gallery. This approach to presenting the works maintains a link to the exhibition space and reproduces the spatial, and sometimes conceptual, relationships between works in the gallery context.

Room One

Patrica Tusa Fels and Don Fels
Shotgun
digital print
2010

The Du Mois Gallery, a shotgun house in the Freret district of New Orleans has become a stimulus of thought for the artist and architect team Patricia Tusa Fels and Don Fels. The Shotgun project collages together images and architectural floor plans as a visual mind-map of Tusa Fels and Fels's thinking process about "the shotgun house as a living portrait of New Orleans" (ET 2010). The artists note that historically "[t]he shotgun house is an indigenous response to the hot humid climate of New Orleans. Despite the passage of many decades and a gauntlet of difficulties, tens of thousands of these houses remain standing in New Orleans. Built as homes to immigrants, former slaves and working class families, the shotguns have continued to provide affordable housing efficiently and gracefully in the city" (ET 2010).

IDEAS

Candy Chang
I Wish This Was
adhesive paper and ink
2010

In this work, Candy Chang placed grids of blank red and white *I Wish This Was* stickers on abandoned buildings, storefronts, and broken sidewalks, along with black ink markers that invited contributions by passersby. The contributions of New Orleans residents were then photographed and posted to a Flickr photo-sharing site. Chang's initial photos were added to by interested members of the community, resulting in a growing archive of wishes for New Orleans neighborhoods. She encourages the ongoing placement of stickers "on abandoned buildings and beyond" (ET 2010), their photo-documentation, and contribution to the Flickr archive.

Within the context of the urban sprawl in a post-Katrina moment, Chang's project offers a starting point for Ethnographic Terminalia visitors to take an experiential piece of the exhibition beyond the gallery space and publicly share their hopes for the revitalization of their community.

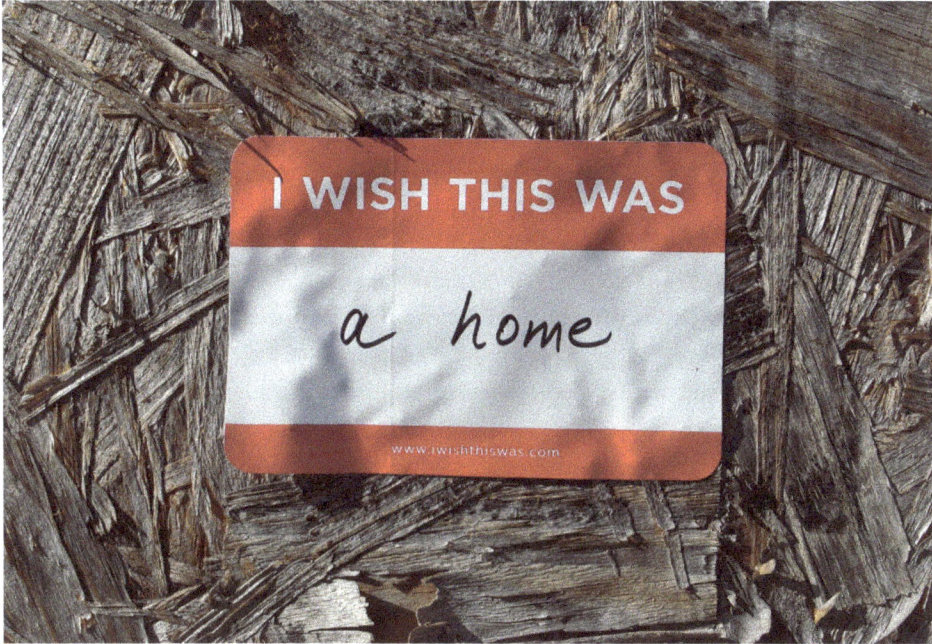

Stephanie Keith
Vodou Brooklyn: Five Ceremonies with Mambo Marie Carmel
photograph/digital prints, book
2009

In Stephanie Keith's *Vodou Brooklyn: Five Ceremonies with Mambo Marie Carmel*, two photographs of intimately framed scenes are hung beside a book. The photographs represent one year of Keith's five-year ethnographic commitment to an American-based Vodou community in Brooklyn. As an anthropologist and photojournalist, Keith's book and photo documentary project epitomizes the intersection between art, anthropology, and her documentary practice. The publication is carefully organized according to the Vodou religious calendar. The photographs are a record of five major public ceremonies that were performed by her informant, Mambo Marie Carmel. For Keith, it is important to focus "on what happens in this single transformed basement hosted by the same Mambo" so that "the reader [or viewer] becomes personally involved with the people in the community through seeing them from ceremony to ceremony" (ET 2010).

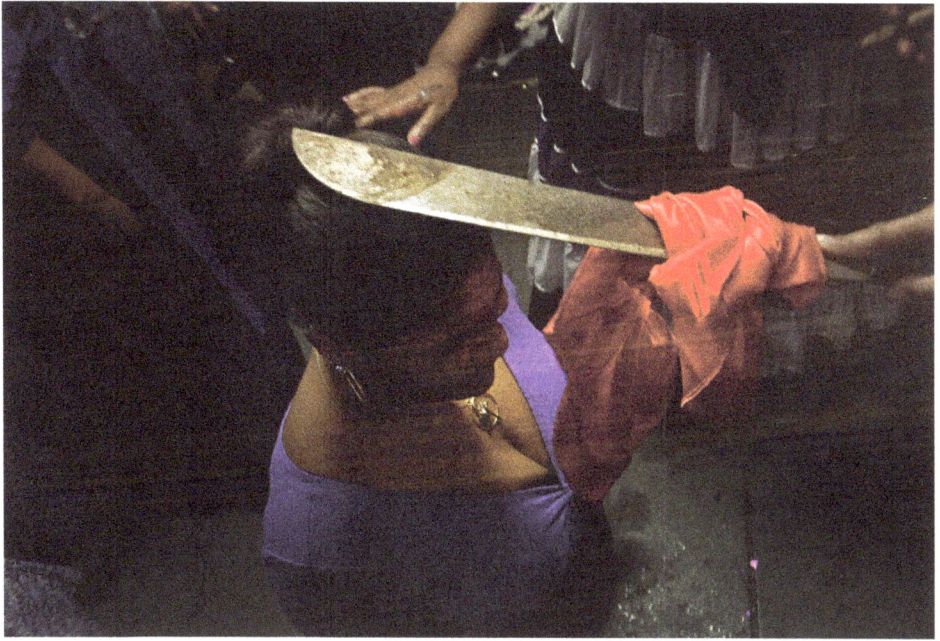

Travis Shaffer
Sorority Skin Tones: A PANTONEs Color Guide
PANTONE© color swatches
2010

Travis Shaffer presents *Sorority Skin Tones: A PANTONE© Color Guide* as a visual ethnography of American sorority circles via online media. This work consists of 20 large-scale PANTONE© color swatches arranged in a grid-like pattern. These color swatches capture Shaffer's methodical research in an artistically conveyed manner. As a methodological approach, Shaffer carried out an exhaustive study using Facebook, where he "analyzed screen captures [and] isolate[d] the necks, faces, chests, arms, legs, foreheads, etc. of 10 popular American sororities via their Official Facebook pages. These screen captures were then averaged and matched to their nearest PANTONE© color. The 20 most frequent matches are illustrated in this work" (*ET* 2010). According to Shaffer, this project was originally imagined as a limited edition, hand-bound book project. Shaffer's work demonstrates the emerging prominence of, and interest in, online fieldwork research for both artists and anthropologists. *Sorority Skin Tones* makes evident the role of new media forums as sites of and for cultural research (http://www.travisshaffer.com).

Simon Rattigan
The Skull Re-Construction Project 2006-08
video
2006-2008

Simon Rattigan's *The Skull Re-Construction Project 2006– 08* is a
documentation of his artistic process whereby he investigates historical
narratives through a creative process of collecting street debris and
constructing new pastiche hominids. Small shards of glass, pottery,
plastic, debris, stone, and concrete collected by Rattigan from the streets
of London are placed on a glass shelf around a video installation of
The Skull Re-Construction Project 2006–08. The video shows Rattigan
at work assembling a skull so that edges of disparate materials meet to
form a new object. These contemporary artifacts, aka waste materials,
as found objects become the so-called "readymade" materials used in
his construction of a human-like skull over a three-month period.
Rattigan notes that "[t]he process [of collection and construction] [is]
at the heart of [his] work [. . .]" (*ET* 2010). Rattigan also notes that
he "began to question the notion of searching for an identity based
on geographical location" that, for him, was generated by the story
of Piltdown man—a "faked fossil find in the south of England that
attempted to place human origins firmly, but fraudulently, in Britain"
(*ET* 2010). For Rattigan, "The Piltdown man became [. . .] an example
of how racial and nationalist discourses [shape] science and in turn
society generally" (*ET* 2010). Rattigan's artistic methodology is infused
with a profound interest in anthropological inquiry that he mediates
through a combination of collage, drawing, video, and sculpture.

Ian Kirkpatrick
Transfer
paper plate, ink
2010

Ian Kirkpatrick takes the mundane and makes it precious through his
series of plates entitled *Transfer* (2010). At a first glance, Kirkpatrick
presents what appear as the iconic Blue Willow or Wedgewood pottery
plates in varied sizes as artifacts one would find in collections such as
the Victoria and Albert Museum in England. Upon closer examination,
the plates reveal themselves as generic Royal Chinet™ paper plates that
Kirkpatrick has bespoke with ink drawings of contemporary pop culture
icons and symbols. Kirkpatrick notes that "[t]his project comprises a
'set' of three plates decorated with visuals derived from traditional blue
and white ceramics, as well as imagery of Islamic, Chinese, Japanese,
Dutch, French, British, and American origin. Together this fusion of
imagery explores the intertwined and complex relationship underlying
the past and present traffic of ideas between East and West" (*ET* 2010).
Kirkpatrick's research-based process further "examines the genealogy of
motifs and fantasies [that are] incorporated into the history of blue-
and-white ceramics" (*ET* 2010). What results from Kirkpatrick's project
is the crossover between how contemporary artists engage with material
culture located in collections around the world and the bridging or
disjuncture between art and artifact
(http://www.iankirkpatrick.ca).

Room Two

Trudi Lynn Smith
Finding Aid: The Pleasure in a Good View
installation (table and stools, photographs, text, file folders, ephemera)
2007

A mixture of photographs, text, drawings, and ephemera, the installation *Finding Aid: The Pleasure in a Good View* is the outcome of artist–anthropologist Trudi Lynn Smith's attempt to precisely relocate the setting of a historical postcard of iconic Banff National Park in Canada. According to Smith, this work is created through highlighting the body in photographic art practice, by "taking archival photographs on a walk to attempt to repeat them as ethnographic investigation and visual art inquiry," and this is an act fueled by the play between the attempt to replicate the photographic act as closely as possible (e.g., through spatial location, time of day, season, camera type, darkroomprocedures) and the revelation that the more the attempt is refined, or the closer one gets, the more distance is felt (*ET* 2010).

In this current installation of *Finding Aid*, a historical photograph and a present-day "repeat" photograph are framed on the wall just above a table that holds an assortment of files. Inside the files, a narrative about the artist and historical photographer is organized on typed index cards and clipped to other photographs she made while trying to repeat the historical postcard. Visitors are invited to sit at the table, and become performers, as Smith writes, "in the subtle act of browsing and shuffling files, sitting and looking, as well as sorting and reading" (*ET* 2010) (trudilynnsmith.blogspot.com).

Nicola Levell and Michael Nicoll Yahgulanaas
SEDUCTION 2010—Into Haida Manga: Raven Kept on Walking
printed panels
2010

Seduction 2010—Into Haida Manga: Raven Kept on Walking is a creation
of Michael Nicoll Yahgulanaas, a Haida artist, and was presented
at Ethnographic Terminalia by Yahgulanaas and Nicola Levell, an
assistant professor in the Anthropology Department at the University
of British Columbia. Ten black-and-white graphic panels are tiled
on the gallery wall in two columns to depict the story of Raven. This
narrative is described by Levell and Yahgulanaas as "the inveterate
trickster of North Pacific Coast indigenous mythology" (*ET* 2010). In
series of panels, Raven twice seduces and tricks a band of fishermen.
In their artist statement, Levell and Yahgualanaas write about how
the unique style that Yahgualanaas created, known as Haida Manga,
"refigures and fuses traditional Haida formlines and iconography
with Japanese-inspired Manga to create a contemporary idiom for
circulating Haida oral narratives and cautionary tales within and
beyond indigenous, local and generational spheres of exchange" (*ET*
2010). The panels were accompanied and contextualized by a short film,
RED (2009) that showed on a small DVD player with headphones. The
collaborative film, directed by Jon Ritchie, presents Yahgulanaas and
documents a five-meter-long mural that Yahgulanaas produced for his
2009 graphic novel, *Red: A Haida Manga* (http://www.mny.ca).

This bird is a guy who hides his third. He tucks it away while he sizes the herd.
So swishy now, he's quite a looker. Came into our town our very first hooker.

Robert Willim and Anders Weberg
Elsewhereness: New Orleans
video
2010

Elsewhereness: New Orleans is the most recent work in a series that
brings together a video by Anders Weberg in collaboration with
sound by Robert Willim to produce an audiovisual work dealing with
questions of site specificity both in art and in anthropology. As the
gallery visitor enters the space, an audiovisual loop shows on a large
flat screen monitor as the sound plays into the gallery space. The work
explores the artists' absence from the locale where the images were
made. Rather than reporting back their experience of place, the work
is based entirely upon audio and video material that the artists glean
from the Internet about the place under examination–New Orleans.
Willim and Weberg note that "the audiovisual pieces are manipulated
and composed into a surreal journey through an estranged landscape,
based entirely on the culturally bound and stereotypical preconceptions
of the artists about the actual location" (*ET* 2010). Images come into
focus and just as they become identifiable they slide away into bands
of color and abstract forms. Likewise, just as the audio representations
of New Orleans become discernible they lift away into a sound track
all its own. *Elsewhereness: New Orleans* forms part of a larger series of
work that includes *Elsewhereness: Utrecht, Elsewhereness: Manchester*, and
Elsewhereness: Yokohama
(http://www.elsewhereness.com).

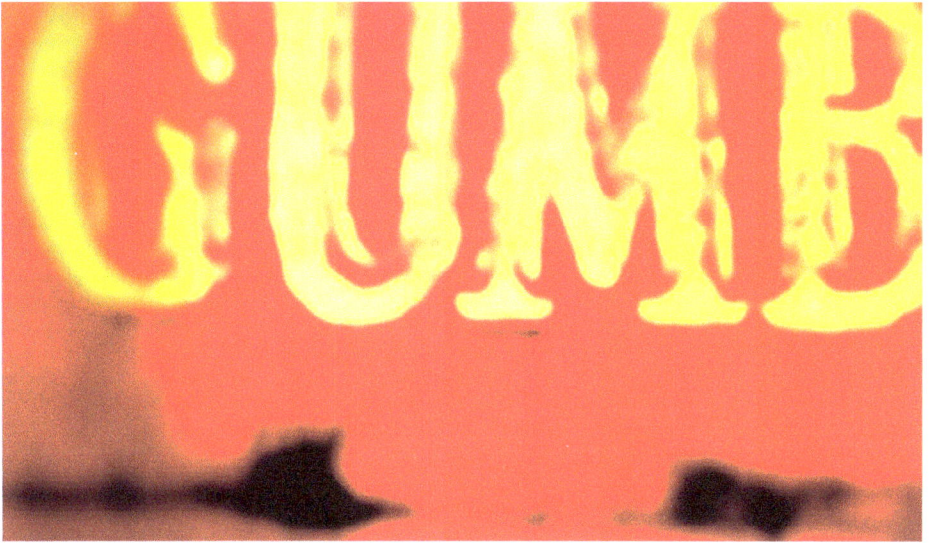

Juan Orrantia
See Ports (Work in Progress)
video
2010

Six black-and-white photographs hang on the gallery wall in a grid structure. This body of work, by photographer and anthropologist Juan Orrantia, documents the space and place of ports. Orrantia writes, "*See Ports* begins after the thrill and romance of ocean travel halts at the pier, when the sounds of waves are shunned by the noises of drills, engines and cranks. It is an evocation of lives caught in a strip of land fenced between the sea and the city, defined by circulation and the frictions of trade" (*ET* 2010). From the photographs, it is impossible to know or contextualize the location of the port as the ocean itself is almost invisible in the images. Instead, these photographs resonate with what is left behind in the movement of goods and caught in Orrantia's camera gaze–vast tracts of sandy land with shipping containers, industrial remnants, tire tracks, bird tracks, fences, piles, pipes leading into the ground, clothes hanging on fences, and workers with protective gear who look startled.

Ahmad Hosni
Go Down, Moses: A Book on South Sinai
photographs, books
2010

A blank book on a stand accompanies a set of three large color photographs with text that hang on the gallery wall. The photographs, by Ahmad Hosni, are a selection of works that were produced over the course of fieldwork carried out during a period of two years in South Sinai. The text plan that is paired with the photographs contains excerpts of writing by Samuel Taylor Coleridge, William Faulkner, and the *Book of Hosea*. Together the text and the blank book form a relationship with the photographs. Within the images, one scene captures a single figure holding a suitcase and looking back at the photographer in the space of what appears to be a tourist mall, while another is situated in a industrial development in the desert, and a third has the wistful gaze of a girl behind a car window. These photographs are taken from Hosni's book project, designed to be a "reflection on the status of a region in the process of becoming a "tourist enclave"" (*ET* 2010). Hosni's color photographs are atypical tourist photographs in that they focus upon place making and the lived realities of what the photographer calls "tourism on the edge" (*ET* 2010). Yet the project never came to fruition as intended. Hosni explains that the book remains blank as it was "de facto censored" by a combination of local and EU organizations that objected to the content and title of the book (http://www .thewhiteboard.info/page/go-down-moses).

To rise before me—Rise, O ever rise,
Rise like a cloud of incense from the Earth!
Thou kingly Spirit throned among the hills,
Thou dread ambassador from Earth to Heaven,
Great Hierarch! tell thou the silent sky,
And tell the stars, and tell yon rising sun
Earth, with her thousand voices, praises God.

Room Three

Fiamma Montezemolo
Bio-Cartography of Tijuana's Cultural-Artistic Scene: The Uterus
as Limit and/or Possibility One Thing and Another Belonging
Machine: Color by Chance.
mixed media
2010

Three works by Fiamma Montezemolo interrogate the notion of border zones—geographic and political borders as well as disciplinary borders. Montezemolo's work engages with a phenomenological approach, inviting participation of the audience to reveal potential and limits of action and agency. In *One Thing and Another* (2010), a constellation of tiny music boxes are attached to the walls and participants are invited to activate the small hand-crank, creating infinite possibilities of sounds. In *Belonging Machine: Color by Chance* (2010), the gallery visitor works a modified slot machine, one that articulates and exposes classificatory categories. In *Biocartography of Tijuana's Cultural-Artistic Scene: The Uterus as Limit and/or Possibility* (2010) imagery of an ultrasound and diagnostic text narrate artistic limitations within the city of Tijuana.

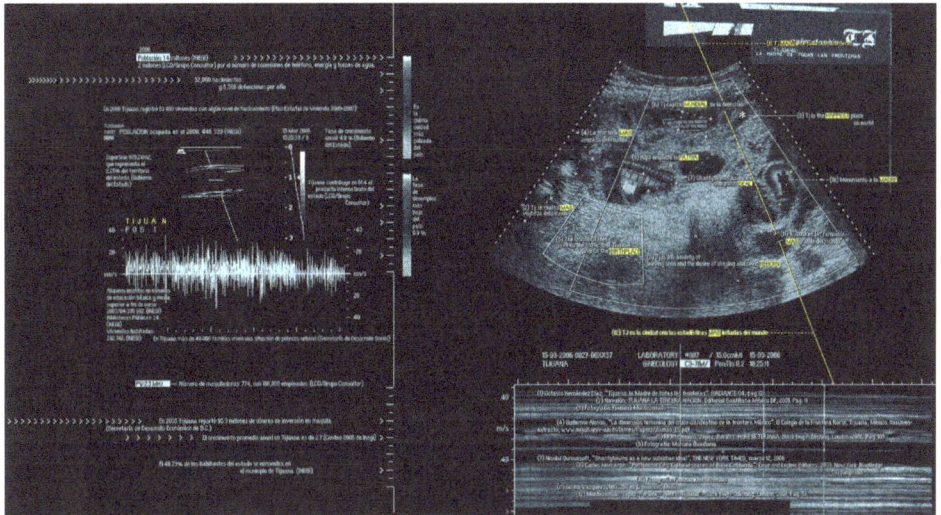

Anthony Callaway
Art(i)fact
drawing on paper
2010

Two small-scale framed works by Anthony Callaway hang as a vertical diptych and are two distinct elements from his larger project entitled *Art(i)fact*. Callaway is an enrolled member of the Karuk Tribe of California, whose artistic practice represents his experience of "[w]orking directly with Karuk objects and information [that has] sparked a [personal] desire [for Callaway] to further explore the various design patterns that embellished baskets and other objects such as bone purses and dance regalia" (*ET* 2010). Callaway's practice is not about mimicking or tracing the patterns that he finds on material culture in museum collections, but rather his artistic goal is to "explore and reinterpret these designs as a contemporary artist of Karuk and Euro-American ancestry" (*ET* 2010). Each piece is meticulously drawn with vibrant red, blue, and green colors that are contrasted against monochromatic shading in a rhythmic pattern that is decontextualized from its original referent. Using his artistic practice to trace out traditional indigenous knowledge stored in objects found in museums, Callaway blurs what he sees as "[. . .] an artificial boundary between traditional and contemporary Native art" (*ET* 2010) (http://www.anthonycallaway.com).

The Un/Natural State of Things
Dada Docot
photographs
2010

The Un/Natural State of Things by Dada Docot comprises five
photographs that are installed in a vertical arrangement in an intimate
space as you enter into Room Three. All but one image is a closely
framed, monochromatic visual memory of old books from Docot's
family's collection. Dada Docot notes that

> *The Un/Natural State of Things* is a series of photographs
> of decomposing books, which were once owned by my
> family members. I focus my lens/attention on old, neglected
> possessions—objects that provide glimpses of my family's
> history. Now bug-infested and severely damaged by frequent
> flooding, these books are among our souvenirs from a long
> time ago, from before we all got caught in this complex world
> of international migration (*ET* 2010).

Currently a Ph.D. Candidate in Anthropology at the University of
British Columbia, Canada, Docot's global migration with her family
and her unique personal experience informs this project as a model of
autoethnography. According to Docot, she is "[l]ooking at migration
as an arena where citizenships and identities are performed, re/ defined
and re/asserted, her photography and film works focus on the intricate
and the intimate" (*ET* 2010)
(http://www.dadadocot.kulturavolunteers.org).

Room Four

Video Salon

Roderick Coover
Det siste utbruddet/The Last Volcano
video
2010

Created after the eruption of Iceland's Eyjafjallajökull volcano in
early 2010, Roderick Coover's video work *Det siste utbruddet/The Last
Volcano* is set in Bergen, Norway. The project places subtitled audio
narratives of Norwegian folktales evoking memory of disaster alongside
slowly revolving video images of the Norwegian landscape—fishing
boats, apartment blocks, evocations of everyday work, and domestic
life. Coover notes that these narratives "return as fragments in light
of the ongoing volcanic eruptions" (*ET* 2010). Coover also notes that,
the video is "the first of a series of works recorded in Norway that
juxtapose folk histories and contemporary events to explore narrative
and associative characteristics of cultural anxieties and collective
memory" (*ET* 2010). *Det siste utbruddet/The Last Volcano* was produced
in collaboration with Scott Rettberg (writer), Gro Jrstad Nilsen (voice),
and Jan Arild Breistein (voice) (http://www.roderickcoover.com).

Kate Hennessy and Richard Wilson
Active Pass to IR9
video
2008

Active Pass to IR9 is a video-based ethnographic collaboration between Kate Hennessy and Richard Wilson, who grew up together on Galiano Island, in British Columbia, Canada. The silent video projection depicts the full length of a road that runs from the ferry terminal at the south end of the island to the Penelekut Indian Reserve #9 at the road's northern terminus. A single unedited shot traces the weaving yellow line that divides the road through a verdant, rain-soaked landscape. Two fields of scrolling text running parallel on either side of the screen represent memories and associations that Kate and Richard each have with this physical space and their individual understandings of place as they move through it together for the first time. The texts are generated from transcripts of their conversation while driving. The content of this conversation spans the scope of raising the question of Aboriginal rights, and the role of fishing in the recognition of rights, and knowledge of family histories. Hennessy and Wilson mobilize video as a tool for experimenting with ethnographic methods, and as a medium for communicating the results (http://www.activepasstoir9.wordpress.com).

They knew
it was their
right to fish,
then they had
to go to court.

Anything can
open the door
a little bit.

Susan Hiller
The Last Silent Movie
video
2007

Susan Hiller's work, *The Last Silent Movie*, employs video in the powerful service of sound and text rather than image. According to Hiller, the work

> opens the unvisited, silent archives of extinct and endangered languages to create a composition of voices that are not silent. They are not silent because someone is listening. The work sets free some of the ghosts and specters haunting the unacknowledged "unheimlich" of sound recording which allows us to hear the words and voices of people mostly now dead. In *The Last Silent Movie*, some of the participants sing, some tell stories, some recite vocabulary lists and some of them, directly or indirectly, accuse us, the listeners, of injustice (*ET* 2010).

The work presents archival recordings of extinct or endangered languages that are enlivened in an act of remediation. The viewer–listener is implicated as witness, and is asked to consider what kind of obligation such implications may create.

Thomas Ross Miller
Radio Iqaluit
video
2008

Thomas Ross Miller's *Radio Iqaluit* is composed of video sequences
of melting ice sheets and glaciers, of flocks of birds disappearing
against a pixelated horizon, and of telephone wires and snowy rooftops
that suggest ongoing human habitation, and dynamic moments
of contact and change in the northern environment. These images
are accompanied by a sound track drawn from short-wave radio
transmissions that are reworked by Miller into an ambient stream
of remixed communication, compression, and distortion. Miller's
juxtaposition of sound and image grab hold of and articulate the
movement of "invisible energies" (ET 2010). This video piece represents
the mining of an atmospheric archive of signal, noise, and image. Miller
positions himself as one cultural producer of many in the colonial
history of relationship making in the north.

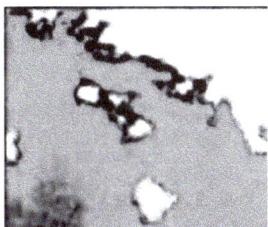
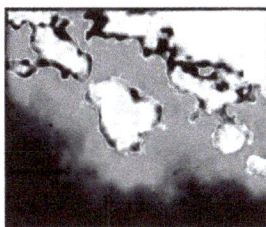

Trish Scott
That Holiday
video
2009

Performance, video, and installation artist Trish Scott brings her
intention to "intervene in and transform experiences of everyday life"
(*ET* 2010) to her video work *That Holiday*. Scott explores the common
act of viewing holiday photographs and reminiscing about shared
experience; however, rather than reviewing images from personal
albums, she presents photographs drawn from "found" photo albums of
three different British couples, who imagine that they themselves are
the holidaying couple in the photographs, and construct improvised
narratives of their imagined holiday. These three audio narratives are
woven together with the found images of the couple in Turkish ruins,
eating a meal, shopping in a market, resting in the shade, and visiting a
zoo, and become almost indistinguishable as the three couples convey
similar responses and use comparable language. According to Scott,
"[t]his piece constitutes part of an ongoing research project into the
cultural constructedness of personal memory objects. Despite the
infinite recodeability of photographs the narratives in this piece diverge.
Whilst each couple draw on their individual experience their comments
and inferences are remarkably similar. This serves to focus attention
on both the ritualistic aspects of holidaying and the specific linguistic
script underpinning the performative recall of holidays via photographic
triggers" (*ET* 2010)
(http://www.trishscott.org).

Stephanie Spray
Untitled
video
2009

Stephanie Spray's video documentation, *Untitled*, captures a 14-minute conversation of a Nepali couple that intends to deliberately upset viewer expectations of linguistic translation in ethnographic media. Spray's camera records an intimate interaction between two "restless" people, who argue, listen, light cigarettes, and obliquely watch a small child, presumably their own; however, the content of their conversation is left open to viewer speculation, and the effect is unsettling. Spray writes that viewers are encouraged to ponder ethical questions regarding the presence of the camera—what it shares and withholds—as well as that of the filmmaker as she hangs around, delving into the lives of her 'subjects' (ET 2010). Spray contends that the viewer becomes a "loiterer" along with the video's subjects.

Room Five

The fifth room of this shotgun house turned art gallery retains the most distinctive aura of its architectural inception—the kitchen. The pieces deployed in this room dialogue with the original structure of the "house," ensnaring vestiges of notions of interior/exterior, public/private, and family/community.

Dona Schwartz
In the Kitchen
photographs
2009

Appropriately placed, Dona Schwartz's series from *In the Kitchen* feature her own ethnographic study of her family as their actions and interactions with their environment and each other are revealed in these deeply personal portraits. For Schwartz, these images, which she first began shooting in 2003, reflect "[...] a range of activities, interactions, and emotions that provide [...] a wellspring for reflecting on the meanings of family, interconnection and individuation. Seen over a range of time, the kitchen offers a view of life's continuities and changes'.'The photographs provide insight into the difficulties of reflexive ethnographic studies invoking the discussion of the "writing culture" moment. Schwartz's images reverberate with its placement here, thus drawing the viewer into careful consideration of both the context of ethnographic investigation and ethnographic display.

Jan Lemitz
Fields of Supply
video
2010

Jan Lemitz's *Fields of Supply* investigates the production of space into place in the Seoul region, focusing on complexity of territoriality, agency, and aesthetics in the form of vacant lots and their transformation into garden spaces. According to Lemitz, these photographs prioritize the use of space since "by turning non-spaces into purpose-made, meaningful and efficient microcosms, they contribute to a micro process of cultural and social progression" (*ET* 2010). Lemitz articulates a challenge in this series as the fabrications of the working class that operates "horizontally" in opposition to the "vertical high-rise" by reframing the landscape through this visual rhetoric (*ET* 2010). These images provide a counter aesthetic through both individual agency and the usevalue of the space. Within Ethnographic Terminalia 2010: New Orleans, the photographs by Lemitz further challenge the boundaries of the delineation of the public/ private and interior/exterior understandings of the socially produced environment (http:// www.janlemitz.com).

Jenn Karson
Scoring the Streets of New Orleans
sound, box, speakers
2010

Jenn Karson's *Scoring the Streets of New Orleans* foregrounds the auditory experience of place. Created for Ethnographic Terminalia 2010 Karson emphasizes the labyrinthine nature of sound as discrete, ephemeral, and mutable. Installed in an exterior corridor of the gallery, recordings of Bourbon Street are projected through speakers and coalesce with the ambient sounds of the gallery environment. This piece privileges sound as a way of knowing, one that emerges as a rhythmic auditory cityscape. The artist writes that "fragments of song float from street corners and weave throughout the open-air bars and restaurants that line Bourbon Street. For the passerby, pieces of numerous songs are threaded into one melody. Time signature is determined by the walker's gate, notes by the chance encounters with the sound events of the place..." (*ET* 2010).

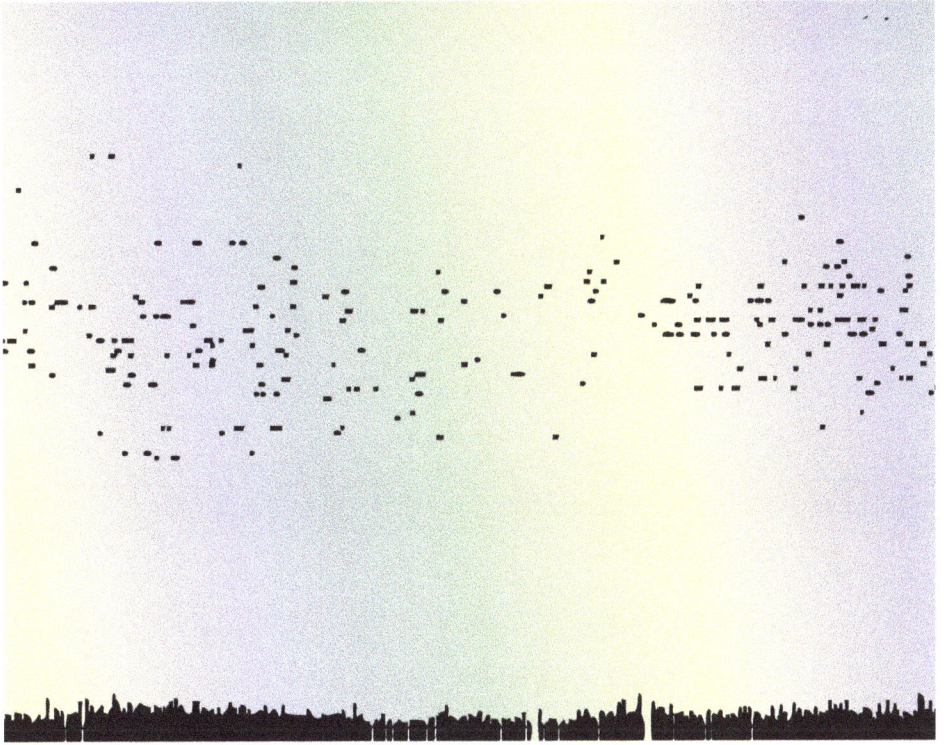

Barrister's Gallery

Barrister's Gallery in New Orleans has been called "a Shaman's Attic," a "twilight zone," and "livingmuseum,' by local visitors and the New York Times. Its location has changed over its 35-plus years to various locations to accommodate its rich and varied vision for ethnographic, outsider, and experimental works. Now, in the St. Claude Arts District, this space also provided homes for the expanding exhibition of Ethnographic Terminalia 2010.

Ryan Burns
Profane Relics
installation (soil)
2009

Ryan Burns's *Profane Relics* is an installation that explores the relationship between people and possession, use and disuse. Towering over the viewer, this sculptural presence entices the viewer to visually excavate those objects deployed by Burns to "tell the story of the past twenty years of war and mineral exploitation in the Democratic Republic of Congo [. . .]" embedded in the ten foot by ten foot matrix of red soil (*ET* 2010). Burns states that his work "examines the traces left behind by time-based processes of growth and history [. . .] explor[ing] the nature of objects both organic and discarded, revealing the implicit stratification of meaning and its myriad interpretations" (*ET* 2010). This installation reminisces about the archaeological process of excavation, in coalescing multiple pasts into the present, not as trace, but as evidence. This evidence narrates a story through the objects embedded in the work, thus operating as a footprint of what has been left behind and revealing bits and pieces in a tumultuous history. When installed, this immense piece overwhelms the viewer as a harbinger of the consequences of a consumer-oriented society
(http://www.profanerelics.wordpress.com).

Lina Dib
Recantorium
video, motion detector
2010

Lina Dib's interactive video, *Recantorium*, (installed at Barrister's Gallery), takes as its subject the accumulation of objects that reflect the personal nature of material culture. Dib explains that in the video "[l]iterally, a heap of objects belonging to local Houstonians—items that people value and keep for various reasons—accumulates or vanishes" (*ET* 2010). Her work encourages the viewer to explore the transient nature of these collections through their own physical movements in the gallery space. With the viewers' movement, the objects on the screen are reconfigured. The interaction of the viewer reveals or reverses the flow of time, as the collection slowly amasses or slowly disappears as they move throughout the space. Dib foregrounds the individuality of meaning and value that these objects are afforded by their owners through an accompanying audio of the personal narratives of the owners.

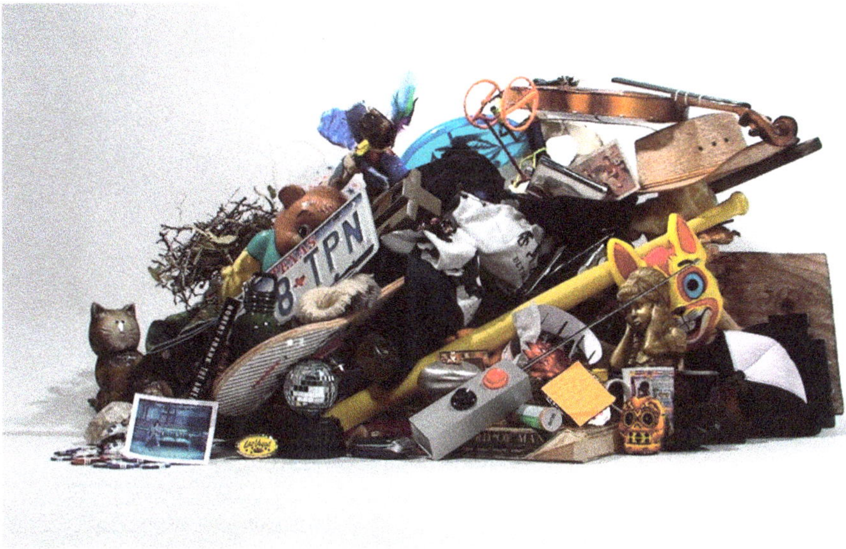
8 TPN

A GALLERY OF PROTOTYPES:
ETHNOGRAPHIC TERMINALIA 2010

Dominic Boyer, Rice University, Houston

No longer content to theorize the ends of the discipline and possibilities of new media, new locations, or new methods of asking old questions, those associated with Ethnographic Terminalia are working in capacity to develop generative ethnographies that do not subordinate the sensorium to the expository and theoretical text or monograph. Ethnographic Terminalia is an initiative designed to celebrate borders without necessarily exalting them. It is meant to be a playful engagement with reflexivity and positionality; it seeks to ask what lies beyond and what lies within disciplinary territories. As an initiative to bring contemporary art practices in closer proximity to forms of anthropological inquiry, Ethnographic Terminalia is primarily concerned with creating opportunities for the exhibition of non-traditional projects.
~Ethnographic Terminalia 2010 Catalog

Boyer, Dominic. 2011 A Gallery of Prototypes: Ethnographic Terminalia 2010, Curated by Craig Campbell, Fiona P. McDonald, Maria Brodine, Kate Hennessy, Trudi Lynn Smith, Stephanie Takaragawa. Visual Anthropology Review 27(1):94-96.

In his review of Ethnographic Terminalia 2009: Philadelphia, Lucian Gomoll's only criticism, a gentle one, concerned the limits imposed by "a serial spatial order that is conventional to art galleries," and he suggested that the curators "might explore the performative and critical potential of looking at alternative histories of exhibition and spatial articulation" (2010:35).

I did not have the pleasure to see Ethnographic Terminalia 2009: Philadelphia, but Ethnographic Terminalia 2010: New Orleans certainly seems to have taken this suggestion to heart. While ET 2009 encamped in the Ice Box Project Space (a massive former walk-in freezer) of Crane Arts, one of the largest contemporary art venues in Philadelphia, ET 2010, although involving more artists (29) and installations (25) than its previous iteration, appeared under more modest circumstances. The exhibit was split across two gallery spaces in New Orleans, the great majority (23) of the installations appearing in a shotgun-style home in the Freret Corridor (Du Mois Gallery) and the other two at Barrister's Gallery in the St. Claude Arts District.

Ethnographic Terminalia seems to me one of the most important and innovative commentaries on the representation of anthropological knowledge to have appeared in the long history of the American Anthropological Association (AAA). Coordinated with, but always at a distance from, the sprawling bazaar that the annual AAA conference has become, Gomoll describes Ethnographic Terminalia well as "an ongoing, collaborative project that features inventive installations by ethnographers, artists, and individuals who might identify as both [which] explore the boundaries of ethnography, challenging traditional disciplinary notions of what we might classify as anthropology or art" (2010:32). I would highlight especially Ethnographic Terminalia's interest in exploring "non-traditional" engagements of the senses and space (physical and conceptual) in the representation of "ethnographic" (I use the term broadly) encounters.

I came away from Ethnographic Terminalia 2010 feeling as though I had toured a gallery of prototypes, of small-scale experimental versions of more complex artifacts to come. In the notoriously difficult section of *The Savage Mind* devoted to François Clouet's representation of Empress Elisabeth's lace collar, Lévi-Strauss writes that all art works "on a diminished scale to produce an image homologous to the object" (1962:24). He contrasts this to the method of science in that the latter would have worked on a real scale, "inventing a loom." Lévi-Strauss emphasizes that the artistic miniature is "not just a diagram or blueprint"; rather, it synthesizes an "intimate knowledge" of the morphology of its objects with "properties that depend on a spatial and temporal context" (25). This method "accentuates some parts and conceals others, whose existence however still influences the rest," leaving the artist "always mid-way between design and anecdote." It would be fair to say that, like Lévi Strauss's miniatures, all the works in Ethnographic Terminalia 2010: New Orleans engage complex problems on a more cognitively and experientially manageable scale, trading the appearance of scientific precision for the exploration of accentuation and concealment. Yet, I would hope that the Ethnographic Terminalia collaborators would share my skepticism that they are therefore stranded "mid-way" between design and anecdote. I saw a much more fertile range of juxtaposition and hybridization here, from photographic flirtations with the "merely" anecdotal to works whose materializations more resembled blueprints and looms. In these borderlands between art and anthropology, the miniatures are obviously restless, pluralizing the modes through which the intimacies of anthropological knowledge can be imagined to communicate. They operate, I would argue, in a prototypical mode, as experimental assemblages of form, function, and effect, designed to provoke new insights and ways of understanding.

There were many examples of these prototypes on display at Ethnographic Terminalia 2010, each with its own methodology and its own sense of audience and impact. Stephanie Spray's video, *Untitled*, which I confess was one of my personal favorites in this show, was marvelously able to capture the 99 percent of life experience—those mundane moments of waiting, boredom, and uncertainty—that comprise no more than one percent of written ethnography. Dona Schwartz's photographic series, *In the Kitchen*, offered provocative glimpses into the complex energy of two families merging. Kate Hennessy and Richard Wilson's road video, *Active Pass to IR9*, explored the processual dialogical negotiation of understandings of place, much as Roderick Coover's *The Last Volcano* treated in anecdotal form the complex interrelationship of landscape and memory. Candy Chang's *I Wish This Was* stickers suggested a different mode of prototype, elegant, and portable, capable of extending the mission of Ethnographic Terminalia beyond galleries and into a variety of creative and personal engagements with cityscapes. Material experimentation was extended in a number of productive directions, for example, Ryan Burns's *Profane Relics*, a powerful archaeological transect of the residues of war and resource exploitation in the *Democratic Republic of Congo*, and Simon Rattigan's *The Skull Re-construction Project*, which assembled and dissembled a human skull made of found materials surviving in the cracks and streets of London. Ian Kirkpatrick's *Transfer* and Nicola Levell and Michael Nicoll Yahgulanaas's *Seduction* experimented very evocatively with aesthetic mash-ups that captured, respectively, the global traffic of images on blue and white ceramic plates and Haida narratives in the graphic form of Manga.

Given the mission of Ethnographic Terminalia to "develop generative ethnographies that do not subordinate the sensorium to the expository and theoretical text or monograph," I was particularly curious about the experiments that sought to move prototypically past more familiar assemblages of vision and sound. These stood out against the majority of works that continued to rely heavily on more established ways of viewing and listening. Like Chang's stickers, the tactility of Fiamma Montezemolo's *Belonging Machine* was remarkably solvent of the norms of audience and thus able to evoke the presence of belonging in a very unique way through its play upon memory, touch, and sound. Lina Dib's *Recantorium* and Trudi Lynn Smith's *Finding Aid* both utilized, although in very different ways, sensitivity to the spatial presence of the audience as an index for communicating memory and meaning. All of these were extremely effective beginnings. My own gentle critique of Ethnographic Terminalia 2010: New Orleans would run something like this: Could reordination of the sensorium not be pushed even farther? Could more be done, for example, with tactility and interactivity in future projects? Could more be done with scent, a sense so central to the experience of anthropological habitation and knowing and yet so absolutely absent from textual, visual, and sonic accounts?

In sum, Ethnographic Terminalia 2010: New Orleans was deliciously paradoxical. At times teasing, at times fulfilling. At times playful, at times somber (especially the minimalist power of Susan Hiller's *The Last Silent Movie*). And then, there was the paradox of a growing abundance of marvelous experimentation miniaturized to the level of a shotgun home. Given the size of Du Mois particularly, I was pleasantly surprised that the environment of the gallery did not produce a sense of confinement. Quite the contrary, it felt exactly like a family home straining to contain its transformational adolescent energy. That energy greeted you at the door, drew you deeper into the convivial sanctums of the family room and kitchen before turning you out into the party in the yard. In this respect, the choice of gallery space and that space's organization proved a marvelous crystallization of the entire intervention. ET 2010 operated very well as a contemplative para-site of AAA 2010, but it also functioned more basically as an escape, a domestic sanctuary from the sensory excess of New Orleans (well documented by Robert Willim and Anders Weberg's *Elsewhereness*) and from the anxiety-inducing corridors of AAA. I can imagine that some visitors might have felt overwhelmed by the informatic density of the New Orleans show and that others might have missed the possibility of larger-scale environmental installations as at Ethnographic Terminalia 2009: Philadelphia. But, in my experience, the gallery of protoypes was an immensely effective and egalitarian curatorial assemblage, one in which quiet corners never felt marginal. Above all, Ethnographic Terminalia 2010: New Orleans was immensely inspirational. As someone who remains very invested in the craft of traditional assemblages of text and voice, Ethnographic Terminalia makes me want to photograph an anecdote, to draw a blueprint, to connect somehow to the fascinating experiments and artifacts that one feels certain are still to come.

References

Gomoll, Lucian
    2010   Ethnographic Terminalia. Visual Anthropology Review 26(1):32–35.
Lévi-Strauss, Claude
    1962   The Savage Mind. Chicago: University of Chicago Press.

www.ingramcontent.com/pod-product-compliance
Lightning Source LLC
Chambersburg PA
CBHW040138270326
41927CB00020B/3435